VETERINARY

ADVICE ON

ARTHRITIS

IN HORSES

Ben Sturgeon
BSc, Cert EP, BVM&S, MRCVS

ABOUT THE AUTHOR

Ben Sturgeon qualified in 1996 and then undertook an internship in large animal medicine at Dublin University. Following that, he headed to Edinburgh University to complete a residency and lectureship in equine medicine and surgery.

Ben currently lives and works in North Yorkshire. In his own words, "Wine, windsurfing and 'Woody' keep him out of trouble.

ACKNOWLEDGEMENTS

Viv Rainsbury: illustrations (page 5). Ben Sturgeon: photography (pages 3, 4, 8, 9, 14, 15, 22, 28, 32, 35). Special thanks from the author: to Lindsay for her inspiration.

**Published by Ringpress Books,
a division of Interpet Publishing,
Vincent Lane, Dorking, Surrey, RH4 3YX, UK.
Tel: 01306 873822   Fax: 01306 876712
email: sales@interpet.co.uk**

First published 2004
© 2004 Ringpress Books. All rights reserved.

ISBN 1 86054 237 9

Printed and bound in Singapore by Kyodo Printing

10 9 8 7 6 5 4 3 2 1

CONTENTS

Introduction

You might have it, you probably know somebody with it – arthritis is an exceptionally common problem. Horses are no different to humans, with lameness and failure to perform both commonly attributable to arthritis. Indeed, arthritis has been recognised as a specific disease entity for decades. In 1829, Turner described it as "ulceration of cartilage", and shortly afterwards "ulcerative disease of the joints" was described as "one of the most frequent, the most grievous, and the most irremediable causes of lameness." To this day it remains one of the most common clinical problems encountered in veterinary practice.

Despite this early recognition, the exact cause, actual biological events occurring in arthritic joints, and agreed best treatment policies remain enigmatic. However, although arthritis is considered incurable, with new techniques of investigation and treatment we are inching our way towards a pain-free and flexible future.

Arthritis can affect any horse.

1 Understanding arthritis

To understand arthritis and the best methods of treatment it is important to appreciate the normal make-up of a healthy joint.

THE EQUINE SYNOVIAL JOINT

Mammalian joints have a common basic structure. The joint comprises articulating bones covered with cartilage that are enclosed within a fluid-filled, two-layered bag. The two layers consist of an inner synovial membrane and an outer, thick joint capsule.

The outer joint capsule is composed of fibrous tissue that contains many joint-supporting ligaments. Together with the capsule, these encompass the enthesis (the joint capsule and ligaments). The inner

Understanding arthritis — side margin

5

THE SYNOVIAL JOINT

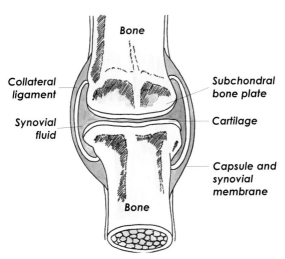

Bone

Collateral ligament

Synovial fluid

Subchondral bone plate

Cartilage

Capsule and synovial membrane

Bone

capsule has a thin layer of synovial cells, and the joint cavity within contains synovial fluid. This fluid is produced by the synovial cells and the joint capsule by filtering blood supplied to the joint.

Synovial fluid contains many components, one of the most important being hyaluronic acid. Hyaluronic acid is vital for maintaining a healthy joint, providing lubrication and nutrition, and it serves a major role in counteracting the compressive forces that are transmitted through a joint. Hyaluronic acid is also a key constituent in articular cartilage.

Cartilage – a smooth, white, spongy tissue – overlies all articulating surfaces, providing a frictionless, gliding surface. It plays a fundamental role in joint structure and function, acting as a shock absorber in distributing compressive forces to surrounding bones via a softer area of bone beneath the cartilage layer known as the subchondral plate. Cartilage is made up of a number of cells, called chondrocytes, that are held together in sheets by collagen (a tough fibrous tissue) and by an amorphous glue. This glue is also vital to withstanding loading on the joint and contains proteoglycans (proteins – specifically chondroitin and keratan sulphate) that bind with hyaluronic acid.

WHAT CAUSES ARTHRITIS?

The joint is a dynamic structure with a regular turnover of all its components and a balanced interaction between each. Interruption or interference with any individual component can result in joint disease. Irrespective of the initial cause, the long-term result is the breakdown of articular cartilage – the hallmark finding in arthritis.

Arthritis can result from acute causes (including joint infection, fractures, and ligament or tendon

CAUSES OF ARTHRITIS

Healthy joint

CHRONIC CYCLIC FACTORS
- Repeated trauma
- Poor joint congruence
- Poor conformation
- Obesity

ACUTE FACTORS
- Loss of stability (fractures, ligament/tendon tears)
- Sepsis
- Inflammation (traumatic synovitis and capsulitis)

SUB-ACUTE FACTORS
- Abnormal matrix formation (congenital disease, degenerative orthopaedic disease, osteochondrosis)

Synovitis and capsulitis

Physical or biochemical damage to articular cartilage and bone

Synovitis/capsulitis, articular cartilage and bone damage

Enzymatic degradation of cartilage

Unhealthy joint (heat, pain and swelling)

disruptions, with resultant joint instability) or chronic problems (such as hard exercise, over many years, which may be exacerbated by factors such as poor foot balance, inadequate training regimens, poor limb conformation, or poor nutrition). Additionally, there

THE UNSEEN EFFECTS OF ARTHRITIS

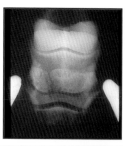

Fracture of the navicular bone.

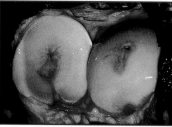

Osteochondrosis affecting cartilage formation in the shoulder.

are some congenital conditions (sub-acute) where there is cartilage dysfunction and the matrix itself does not form adequately during growth, predisposing the joint to trauma. These diseases come under the umbrella term 'developmental orthopaedic disease', and include conditions such as club foot, osteochondrosis (OCD), and Wobbler's. In practice, a combination of factors are often involved and no single inciting cause can be consistently identified.

Irrespective of the causal insult, damaged tissues begin leaking fluid, blood cells and destructive enzymes into the joint. The enzymes degrade proteoglycans and hyaluronic acid, which inhibit the normal growth of cartilage and further stimulate the production of destructive enzymes. The result is a poor-quality synovial fluid, with reduced viscosity and lubrication, and depressed cartilage nutrition. More seriously, direct destruction of cartilage matrix results in swelling and splitting of the smooth layer, exposing

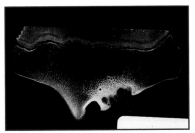

Histological slice of an osteoarthritic joint, showing marked destruction of the subchondral plate and cyst formation.

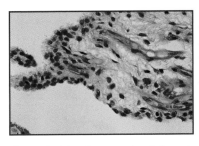

This histological specimen of synovium from an osteoarthritic stifle shows fibrosis and inflammation.

the underlying bone so that it loses its protection from compression.

Without protection, shock absorption by the subchondral bone plate is compromised and the ability to bear weight pain-free is hampered.

Where there is no known direct event causing arthritis, overuse may be to blame. Repetitive work results in compression of the subchondral plate, causing a gradual stiffening and a loss of the shock-absorption capacity. This subjects the articular cartilage to the huge mechanical effects of loading during exercise, resulting in abnormal stresses being placed on the joint and enthesis (the joint capsule and ligaments).

Whether arthritis has resulted from injury, overuse, or a congenital problem, the result is the same – a painful and inflamed joint, a reduction in performance, and a condition that, once started, will not stop with rest alone.

2 Diagnosing arthritis

The clinical signs shown by a horse suffering from arthritis will depend on which joint or joints are affected. If a limb joint is affected, lameness or poor performance would be typical. Classically, this type of lameness improves with rest but worsens with exercise. Alternatively, lameness may be insidious in onset, becoming manifest over many months or years.

If joints other than those in the limbs are involved, pain and loss of function of that joint are found. For example, arthritis of the jaw/skull joint (temporomadibular joint) or of the skull/spine joint (atlanto-occipital joint) results in eating difficulties or in reduced head movement respectively. However, these are relatively uncommon and the usual presentation is a lame horse.

The severity of lameness is not a good indicator of the joint involved, or of the degree of disease. However, it is one of the first clinical signs that result in a veterinary surgeon being called. It is important to consult your vet as soon as possible if you suspect arthritis, as early diagnosis can help with the management of the disease.

INITIAL DIAGNOSIS

On presentation, the vet will physically examine the horse to identify the presence of lameness or pain associated with a diseased joint. Anaesthetic tests may then be carried out to confirm the precise area of disease. To achieve this, a vet may inject local anaesthetic either into a diseased joint or around the nerves supplying the joint (nerve blocking). This freezes the nerves in that joint, eliminating feeling. A lame horse should then become 'sound'.

Testing using anaesthetic is essential for two reasons:

1 Prognosis and treatment varies depending on the joint affected, so careful identification of the joint involved is vital.

2 Once the joint causing pain is identified, a diagnosis of arthritis is largely dependent upon use of radiography and X-rays. However, these have limitations. Firstly, arthritis is a disease of cartilage, and X-rays only visualise bone. As a result, reliance on anaesthetic tests (and other diagnostic modalities) is vital. Secondly, once arthritis has progressed sufficiently, with actual articular cartilage and synovial fluid degradation, a joint will lose its ability to absorb compressive forces. The result is extra bone production around the affected joint, in an attempt to stabilise it, reduce further movement, and prevent ongoing injury. This new bone is called enthesophytes, and it is this we see on X-rays. However, enthesophytes can be present in some normal horses without arthritis, hence the use of anaesthetic tests to confirm whether such enthesophytes are in fact of significance. A further important point is that X-rays are not only important in diagnosis, but also in excluding other differential diagnoses, such as chip fractures and developmental diseases.

RADIOGRAPHIC SIGNS OF DJD

As highlighted above, the use of anaesthetic tests will indicate which joint needs to be visualised. In arthritis, radiography is probably the most important non-

OSTEOARTHRITIC CHANGES SEEN ON RADIOGRAPHS

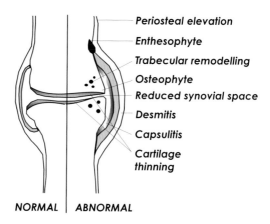

Periosteal elevation

Enthesophyte

Trabecular remodelling

Osteophyte

Reduced synovial space

Desmitis

Capsulitis

Cartilage thinning

NORMAL | ABNORMAL

invasive technique used and deserves a little elaboration.

Thinning of the joint space, osteophytosis, enthesiopathy, changes in subchondral bone, increased synovial fluid and synovial thickening, all provide radiographic evidence of arthritis. Of these, however, only thinning of the joint space actually represents direct evidence of loss of articular cartilage, the salient event in arthritis. The remaining changes provide indirect evidence of cartilage loss and are often inconsistent with the clinical presentation. Many of the lesions observed on radiographs do not cause pain or lameness.

THINNING OF THE JOINT SPACE

X-rays of joints are generally made while the horse is bearing weight. During weight-bearing, the normal synovial joint is separated by two layers of cartilage. On X-rays, the joint space is a dark (radiolucent) line between the opposing bones, and it is a guide to cartilage thickness. Therefore, measurement of the joint space can be used to assess its loss. In arthritic joints, this space is often reduced.

OSTEOPHYTOSIS

Osteophytes are intrasynovial deposits of new bone at the margin of joints. They are the result of inflammatory-mediated activation of cells located at the ends of bones. These cells secrete a cartilage matrix that undergoes endochondral ossification to form a bony osteophyte. During early arthritis, osteophytes are small, but they become larger and denser as the disease progresses. Although osteophyte production is often a reliable sign of disease, it is a secondary change, so its presence does not reflect the disease severity.

ENTHESOPATHY

Enthesis are sites of attachment of joint capsules, tendons and ligaments to bone. Pathological changes in entheses are generally known as enthesopathy and produce enthesophytes. These are bony spurs in the fibro cartilage of entheses, and may be associated with disease. They differ from osteophytes in that they are outside the synovia and they are not, therefore, always associated with disease.

SUBCHONDRAL BONE SCLEROSIS

A less common finding in arthritis, subchondral bone sclerosis represents diseased subchondral bone that has disintegrated due to increased bone turnover. This results in cyst formation in the articular margins.

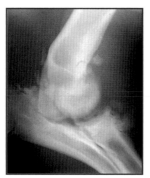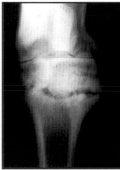

Severe osteoarthritis of high-range (left) and low-range (right) joints. Note the enthesophyte and osteophyte formation. The low-range joint also demonstrates subchondral sclerosis and variable joint space.

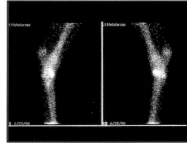

Diagnostic techniques: Pictured left is an ultrasonographic view of a meniscal tear in the stifle of a horse with osteoarthritis. The picture on the right shows 'hot spots' in a horse's hock, as seen with scintigraphy.

SOFT-TISSUE CHANGES

Increased synovial fluid and synovial membrane thickening may both be seen on an X-ray. However, there are several conditions (i.e. sepsis and developmental disease) that can cause distension, so other diagnostic modalities need to be used.

FURTHER DIAGNOSTIC METHODS

At the present time, local anaesthetic tests, followed by radiographic investigation, is the standard method when it comes to diagnosing arthritis. However, other diagnostic and investigative modalities may be used in some cases.

ULTRASONOGRAPHY

Ultrasonography uses sound waves to create an echo image of underlying tissues. Its major advantage is that it is very useful for assessing cartilage, as well as for visualising fractures, infection, OCD and the effects of arthritis.

Ultrasonography is also extremely useful for examining supporting soft-tissue structures around joints. If soft-tissue structures are damaged, they can predispose to arthritis (i.e. tendon tears and stifle meniscal injuries). The main disadvantage of ultrasonography is its lack of sensitivity – negative findings do not necessarily mean there are no other signs of disease.

SCINTIGRAPHY

Scintigraphy (bone scanning) is becoming increasingly available. It relies on the increased uptake of radioactively-labelled cells in areas of excessive bone turnover. The subsequent increased level of radiation at the diseased area is detected by means of a 'gamma camera'. The technique is pain-free and transient low levels of radiation are used. Despite its usefulness, scintigraphy is perhaps best used to localise obscure lameness if standard radiographic examination is inconclusive, where injuries cannot be satisfactorily radiographed, or in horses where standard diagnostic methods cannot be performed.

ARTHROSCOPY

Arthroscopy ('key-hole' surgery) of joints is a routine procedure in human orthopaedics, and it has also been successful in equine orthopaedics over the last 30 years. The technique provides excellent, direct visualisation of the articular cartilage surface, allowing accurate diagnosis and providing better prognostic information.

Arthroscopy is also an excellent means of treatment for many diseases, including removal of chip fractures, treatment of developmental disorders, treatment of bone cysts, and lavage of septic joints. In arthritic joints, flushing the joint to remove inflammatory enzymes and debris may be of great advantage in some cases. The main disadvantage is that a general anaesthesia is required to undertake the examination.

SYNOVIAL FLUID EVALUATION

Synovial fluid evaluation is vital where joint sepsis is suspected. In arthritis, there are many tests available to evaluate the quality of the fluid but they are rarely used, except in experimental circumstances, because of the better methods of diagnosis mentioned above.

OTHER TECHNIQUES

- **Thermography:** This technique may demonstrate changes in surface temperature that relate to the acute (increased thermal emission) and chronic (decreased thermal emission) inflammatory phases of arthritis.
- **Computer tomography (CT) and magnetic resonance imaging (MRI):** These are the current gold standard, providing vastly superior anatomic information and image contrast. Unfotunately, these techniques are not widely available at present.

3 Types of arthritis

Once a diagnosis of arthritis has been made, the vet will progress to identifying the type of disease involved. There are three main types of arthritis:
- Arthritis
- Osteoarthritis
- Degenerative joint disease.

Although similar, the differences are important to appreciate, as prognosis and treatment varies for each.

ARTHRITIS

Arthritis is a term used to describe any inflammatory condition involving a joint. It may be caused by any trauma, from infection to fracture.

OSTEOARTHRITIS

Osteoarthritis is a specific term describing permanent and progressive deterioration of articular cartilage. A diagnosis of osteoarthritis is normally based on radiographic evidence of bone change.

Osteoarthritis is described as primary when its causes are not identified, and secondary when the causal factors can be demonstrated. This is the most common arthritic syndrome in the horse, and this definition is used almost exclusively.

DEGENERATIVE JOINT DISEASE

This term covers both primary and secondary osteoarthritis. Although the central feature of osteoarthritis is loss of articular cartilage, this may not happen initially. Similarly, not all articular cartilage absence or loss leads to osteoarthritis.

OSTEOARTHRITIS IN HORSES

Osteoarthritis in horses can be further classified according to the joint involved and the predisposing factors. The categories are:

- Ostoearthritis of joints with a high range of movement (i.e. fetlock, stifle and elbow), where disease is induced by repetitive overextension and loading of the joint.
- Osteoarthritis of low-motion, high-load joints, which occurs in the pastern in 'ring bone' and in the lower hock joints in 'bone spavin'.
- Osteoarthritis developing secondary to predisposing factors (e.g. articular fractures, joint infections, OCD) and occurring in any joint.
- Non-progressive cartilage erosions, found incidentally during examination of the cartilage and where no cause is identified.

Although such classifications are of value, it is of greater relevance to determine what osteoarthritic conditions you, as an owner, are likely to experience with your horse. The classification system does provide some clues to this. For example, if you are involved in high-performance horses (racehorses), the repetitive high-speed work, on a potentially still developing equine skeleton, predisposes the high-motion joints to damage. The common areas of damage in racehorses are the carpus (knee), either at the level of the radius or in the small articulating bones within the knee (specifically the third carpal bone), and the fetlock. In such cases, cartilage damage and subchondral degeneration can not only induce arthritis but can also precede fracture formation.

Conversely, osteoarthritis of low-motion joints can occur in any horse, although heavier, cold-blooded horses are more prone. The low-motion joints are the shock-absorption apparatus in a horse's leg, and so any horse that has worked steadily may present with such a disorder later in life.

The third classification is the easiest to understand. Trauma may affect any joint and so initiate osteoarthritis, but a second example of this would be in show horses, where maximal growth is desirable. This can be a causal factor in developmental orthopaedic disease (osteochondrosis) and may predispose to osteoarthritis.

TREATMENT GUIDE

The division of cases into these classifications is of further relevance when treatment is considered. In cases where an inciting cause is identifiable (OCD, fracture), treatment is primarily directed at these. Where disease involves high-load, low-motion joints, therapy is aimed at encouraging the normal body response of bone production in an attempt to achieve fusion (ankylosis) of the joint, and so stability.

However, in high-motion joints, no amount of new bone will result in fusion and will only prove detrimental to the joint. This is where the crux of therapy for osteoarthritis lies.

In such cases, the treatment aim is to return the joint environment to normal as soon as possible, halting the detrimental effects of inflammation on the cartilage and synovium. In medical terms this is called 'chondroprotection' – protection of the cartilage chondrocytes.

4 Medical treatments

Treatment of any joint insult should be directed at the initiating cause and then at the secondary, inflammatory consequences.

Flushing out an infected joint, repairing a fracture, or supporting a limb with a tendon injury, are obvious requirements. However, good nursing management is of equal importance.

The use of cryotherapy – ice packs or cold hosing – is common in human sports medicine, and the benefits should not be ruled out for horses. Any acute injury should be iced or hosed for at least 10 minutes, to reduce swelling and bleeding in the area. This protocol should be continued for 72 hours. After this time, heat can be used to reduce stiffness and pain, as well as to improve blood supply to the area. Again, this can be implemented for a further three to five days.

After treating the initial trauma, the long-term outlook needs to be addressed. Regardless of whether cartilage damage has been caused by the injury directly, as the result of an injury, or it is associated with wear and tear, the therapies are similar. They revolve around exercise, correction of abnormal conformations, medical treatments and surgery.

REST AND EXERCISE

Rest, either alone or in conjunction with other forms of therapy, has been recommended for the treatment of osteoathritis for years. Stall rest is frequently advocated by vets for the treatment of lameness.

Unfortunately, confinement is considered detrimental to cartilage defects (total joint immobility leads to cartilage thinning), and exercise is beneficial in maintaining normal concentrations of proteoglycans within the cartilage and actually improving the quality of synovial fluid. However, the converse is also true – excessive exercise on an injured or diseased joint can be equally damaging.

The compromise is 'passive exercise', where the level of rest and *controlled* exercise is carefully planned. Typically, a horse with mild osteoarthritis may be boxed for one week. This would be followed by an in-hand walking exercise programme (from the box), running for up to 60 days, with re-evaluation at intervals during this time. Once an appropriate level of exercise has been attained, the intensity of exercise may be increased. Work levels can be built up similarly until a desired level is attained without loss of performance. Once this desired exercise level has been achieved, a maintenance programme of exercise, along with good equine husbandry and training, should be all that are necessary to keep the horse working long term.

FEET AND CONFORMATION

Equally as important as controlled exercise, foot conformation plays a vital role in the management of arthritis. 'No foot, no horse' is the coined phrase, and it is all too commonly overlooked. An abnormal foot shape results in alteration of the whole limb dynamic. The movement and flight through the air of the limb changes, and the resultant loading forces through the limb are abnormal, which may exacerbate or induce joint disease. By far the best approach to foot conformation is to get your vet and farrier together to

No foot, no horse! Poor foot (left) and limb (right) conformation are predisposing factors to arthritis and can exacerbate the disease. Enlist the help of your vet and farrier to ensure that your horse's feet are kept in tip-top condition. Even if your horse already has arthritis caused by poor conformation, a well-thought-out management plan can help significantly.

discuss any changes. In cases of osteoarthritis that involve joints within the hoof (such as the coffin joint and navicular bone), farrier attention is vital to the successful management of the condition. In such cases, support for the heels is vital to reduce the compressive forces that compound this area initiating and propagating the disease.

MEDICAL THERAPIES
Medical therapy aims to control inflammation in the joint while exercise and remedial farriery are initiated. Therapy revolves around the use of three main groups of drugs:
- Non-steroidal anti-inflammatory drugs (NSAIDs)
- Steroids
- Oral or injectable joint supplements.

NON-STEROIDAL ANTI-INFLAMMATORY DRUGS

Non-steroidal anti-inflammatory drugs (NSAIDs) are commonly used in both human and veterinary medicine. Examples include aspirin, paracetamol, and ibuprofen. In horses, the standard NSAID is phenylbutazone, which has been used for more than 30 years.

NSAIDs are used for their pain-killing, anti-fever and anti-inflammatory effects. They are particularly useful for managing pain when an acute injury occurs, and for allowing exercise and reducing articular inflammation in cases of chronic osteoarthritis.

Whether NSAIDs act predominantly as anti-inflammatories or as pain killers is unknown, but their analgesic effects are vital in maintaining joint mobility by allowing pain-free exercise.

A common concern of owners is that, in chronic osteoarthritis, the use of a NSAID may encourage excessive use of a diseased joint, resulting in further cartilage erosion and joint degeneration. While increased use of an injured joint may lead to further cartilage erosion, normal cartilage requires loading (i.e. exercise) to remain healthy. Furthermore, mobility can prevent fibrosis of the synovial membrane and joint capsule, which significantly reduces joint function. So despite the possible problems, the benefits of improved mobility provided by NSAIDs outweigh the potential problems.

The compromise is that NSAIDs should be used judiciously. Low-level therapy, or treatment given only when the horse is required to undertake exercise, used in combination with an accurate diagnosis and other recommended ancillary treatments (treatment directed at the primary cause, controlled exercise and/or articular medications), is the appropriate course of action.

NSAIDs AND SIDE EFFEECTS

Many owners are concerned about administering drugs over long periods because of potential side effects. There is no such thing as a totally safe drug, and we must all be aware of the potential side effects involved with any treatment we give our animals.

Most NSAIDs, including phenylbutazone, have a narrow safety margin – that is, it is easy to overdose. Moderate doses may be tolerated over long periods, whereas a high dose may cause severe signs of toxicity after a short period of use. Signs of toxicity include stomach and colon ulceration (presenting as colic, diarrhoea or weight loss), kidney problems (presenting as weight loss or excessive drinking/urination), and possible bleeding. This can happen because NSAIDs inhibit two enzymes known as COX 1 and COX 2.

COX 1 is known as the 'housekeeper', helping to regulate normal healthy balances within certain bodily organs. COX 2 is involved in inflammation. Most side effects can be attributed to the inhibition of COX 1 (inhibition of COX 2 is beneficial in injury). Research is currently developing NSAIDs that primarily inhibit COX 2, as these would have all the therapeutic effects of classical NSAIDs without the side-effects. Most NSAIDs available currently are non-selective inhibitors of COX1 and COX2. Carprofen is the only NSAID with demonstrable selectivity. Despite this, practical and clinical advantages afforded by such NSAIDs have yet to be demonstrated in horses.

Despite the possible problems associated with NSAIDs, side-effects are rare when drugs have been administered at correct doses. Reported cases of toxicity are normally due to overdosing, often in ponies, or in cases of colic where several different NSAIDs have been administered over a short period.

NSAIDs AND COMPETITION HORSES

NSAIDs are banned in the vast majority of equine competitions, and many organisations routinely test for such compounds. Historically, salicylate (aspirin) was used by competitors because of its natural occurrence in foods. However, abuse of this loop hole has led to the practice being made illegal by governing bodies (Federation Equine International and The Jockey Club). NSAIDs are not banned outside of competition, but there are no guidelines available giving safe withdrawal times for drugs prior to competition. In such circumstances, the simple answer is not to use them.

NSAIDs AND EUROPEAN LAW

In June 2004, new legislation was introduced that required all horses, ponies and other equines in England to have a passport. Scotland, Wales and Northern Ireland will be introducing similar legislation. The introduction of this legislation will bring the UK in line with European legislation.

The legislation underpins a robust control system to ensure that horses treated with veterinary medicines not authorised for use in food-producing animals, cannot be slaughtered for human consumption. Moreover, it will allow the UK horse industry to continue to use such medicines on horses not intended for the human food chain.

STEROIDS

Corticosteroids were first used in the management of equine osteoarthritis in 1955, and have remained a major therapy ever since. They have multiple effects within the joint. They inhibit the inflammatory cascade as well as inhibiting many other inflammatory effects, such as the release of degradative enzymes. Despite these advantages, a lot of publicity revolves around the negative effects of corticosteroids, such as suppression of cartilage metabolism, and inhibition and depletion of proteoglycan and hyaluronic acid (although this normally happens only when steroids are used at high doses). The term 'steroid arthropathy' has arisen to describe these supposed complications. Paradoxically, however, it has been shown that, at very low doses, steroids can significantly help damaged cartilage.

Despite these conflicting pieces of experimental information, corticosteroids demonstrate potent relief for traumatised and inflamed joints. There are several indications for their use in joint disease. Firstly, a single injection of a short-acting corticosteroid may be used in cases of acute inflammation (synovitis) in high-motion joints where there is no radiographic evidence of osteoarthritis. The aim of this is to reduce inflammation as quickly as possible.

Secondly, longer-acting corticosteroids may be used in higher doses to provide pain relief. For example, in low-motion joints (such as in the treatment of bone spavin), corticosteroid injections can allow the horse to work pain free, so accelerating the fusion of these joints. In such cases, treatments may be repeated periodically (according to your veterinary surgeon's advice) in order to maintain a working animal.

PROBLEMS WITH STEROIDS

Despite the advantages of using steroids, their use remains somewhat controversial. The profound symptomatic relief provided by intra-articular injection of steroids can mean that some owners use their animals before the joint has become sufficiently stable. This results in the acceleration of joint degeneration rather than the halting of it. Furthermore, if steroids are administered when there has been no attempt to treat the primary cause of arthritis – such as a chip fracture – the result will be a rapid progression of osteoarthritis rather than any improvement.

Combined with an adequate rest period and training programme, steroids are certainly beneficial in returning high-motion joints to a normal synovial environment. Therefore, it is essential to follow your veterinarian's advice on the other elements of arthritis management, such as rest and exercise (see page 20).

Presently, intra-articular use of steroids are best reserved for two sorts of patient:

- Cases of acute joint inflammation in high-motion joints, where intra-articular fractures and ligament injuries are not present and where therapy must be accompanied by a period of rest.
- In the treatment of osteoarthritis in low-motion joints, where the aim is to allow pain-free exercise so that fusion is accelerated.

To avoid inappropriate use, necessary precautions include radiographing the joint and always following an injection into a high-motion joint with at least 30 days' rest.

Many owners are concerned that corticosteroids may induce laminitis. This is a risk with any steroid treatment, but it should be remembered that the doses used in osteoarthritis therapy are generally small, so the likelihood of iatrogenic (vet-induced) disease is minimal. That said, if your horse or pony has a condition predisposing to laminitis (such as Cushing's disease), has had previous laminitic episodes, or is obese, caution should be advised when using corticosteroids.

ORAL & INJECTABLE SUPPLEMENTS

The aim of osteoarthritis therapy is to sustain chondrocyte metabolism while inhibiting inflammatory enzymes (i.e. chondroprotection). There are two supplements that achive this, sodium hyaluronate and polysulphated glycosaminoglycans.

SODIUM HYALURONATE

This is a glycosaminoglycan, and, therefore, a normal component of articular cartilage, synovial fluid and synovial membrane. It has been used in the treatment of equine osteoarthritis for more than 20 years. It improves both lameness and synovial fluid quality.

Sodium hyaluronate may be administered by intra-articular or intravenous routes, the latter being the preferred choice where multiple joints are involved. However, the intra-articular route is the most commonly used in cases of acute joint inflammation before there are radiographic changes suggestive of osteoarthritis. The rationale for this is that, although there is no primary chondroprotection or support for the cartilage, sodium hyaluronate will be beneficial to the cartilage in a number of ways. These include reducing synovial inflammation, scavenging free radicals, and acting as a lubricant to prevent adhesion formation during synovial inflammation. The protocol for its use is a weekly injection in combination with a gradually increasing exercise regime. This should be followed until the animal is either sound, or fails to improve following two consecutive injections.

POLYSULPHATED GLYCOSAMINOGLYCANS

PSGAGs are a semi-synthetic preparation of glycosaminoglycan. They were developed following observation of proteoglycan depletion from cartilage

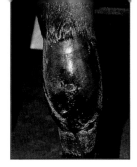

Intra-articular administration of PSGAGs is normally combined with antibiotics, to minimise the risk of the horse developing joint sepsis (pictured left).

in diseased joints. Like sodium hyaluronate, PSGAGs have been shown to be effective in reducing lameness and inflammation in cases of joint disease, as well as in slowing the progression of osteoarthritis. It achieves this by inhibiting inflammatory enzymes and by stimulating the synthesis of both hyaluronan within the joint and proteoglycans within articular cartilage.

PSGAGs can be administered intra-muscularly (where multiple joints are affected) or intra-articularly. Occasional cases of bleeding into the joint and joint sepsis have been seen following their intra-articular use. As a result, intra-articular antibiotics are commonly combined with PSGAGs on administration.

Despite this serious potential consequence, it is important to stress that any intra-articular therapy increases the potential of sepsis, and may cause joint trauma. Horses should receive intra-articular therapy *only* under strictly controlled and aseptic conditions.

PSGAGs are used predominantly in cases where osteoarthritis is visible radiographically. They may be supplemented with corticosteroids for joint effusions with no evidence of radiographic degeneration, or with sodium hyaluronate for mild osteoarthritis. Equally, because of the possible consequences when used intra-articularly, it is more common to use these drugs intramuscularly, or to follow a single intra-articular dose with a minimum of 5-7 intra-muscular injections.

ORAL JOINT SUPPLEMENTS

There are a large number of oral preparations of glycosaminoglycans available for use in horses. Examples include chondroitin sulphate (Flex Free) and combinations of chondroitin sulphate and glucosamine hydrochloride (Cosequin). These compounds are sold as 'nutraceuticals' rather than as pharmacological agents, and, as a result, they have not been subjected to rigorous assessment for veterinary use. This may account for their extravagant medicinal claims.

Glucosamine is a basic constituent of glycosaminoglycans. Experiments have demonstrated enhanced cartilage synthesis following administration. In comparison, studies with chondroitin sulphate show a limited stimulatory effect and limited anti-inflammatory effects. However, clinical trials using chondroitin over six weeks in lame horses have demonstrated improved flexion and reduced lameness.

A second issue is whether they are actually absorbed from the intestine. Human trials have demonstrated symptomatic improvement following oral administration, but no equine experiments currently support this. Despite this, there is anecdotal evidence for beneficial results following their use.

Consequently, the best preparation to use is open to question, and will depend on the individual horse. In most cases, the ideal is a combination of the two key ingredients over a long treatment period, with other treatment modalities (exercise management and foot conformation) included.

A final note on the subject is the use of shark cartilage as a joint supplement. We must consider the ethical questions behind using products obtained from a protected species when synthetic alternatives are available.

5 Surgical treatments

S urgical techniques for joint problems have made considerable advances in recent years, internal fixation of fractures and arthroscopy surgery being foremost. These significantly reduce the degree of pathology in an injured joint, and so prevent or reduce the severity of osteoarthritis after an injury.

INDICATIONS FOR SURGERY

The primary surgical indication is normalisation of the joint interior and prevention of osteoarthritis. Once articular cartilage degeneration is established, surgery cannot reverse the damage.

Surgery undertaken to prevent osteoarthritis after a trauma may include:

- *Fragment removal* when an isolated bone fragment or cartilage exists within a joint and interferes with normal function.
- *Removal of surface defects* to reduce joint irritation.
- *Internal fixation and joint reconstruction* to establish normal joint anatomy where there are articular defects with fractures.
- *Lavage* (flushing) to remove infection and the inflammatory by-products in sepsis.
- *Soft-tissue debulking* (removal) where trauma causes proliferation of soft-tissue structures (i.e. fetlock synovial masses).
- *Arthrodesis* (fusion) of a joint where trauma or degeneration is so advanced that normal function cannot be re-established and movement continually initiates pain.

Before any surgery is undertaken, it is important to balance the pros and cons. The horse's age, the number of joints affected, the predicted horse's workload once treatment is completed, your future expectations, anaesthetic risks, cost factors, etc. Each of these factors must be carefully discussed with your vet. Although surgery can achieve remarkable results, each case must be considered on its own merits and surgery will not be suitable for all cases.

ARTHROSCOPY

The mainstay for the majority of surgery is arthroscopy – 'key hole' surgery utilising optic-fibre cameras and minute instruments.

The primary advantages of arthroscopy, both diagnostically and therapeutically, are the greatly enhanced accuracy with which the majority of joint structures can be evaluated. For example, arthroscopy has identified that loss of up to 30 per cent of cartilage cover from individual carpal (knee) bones does not result in a reduction in prognosis. However, when there is more than 50 per cent loss of articular cartilage, or a significant loss of subchondral bone, there is a significant decrease in the number of horses returning to perform successfully. Such information is impossible to predict from X-rays. Also, because

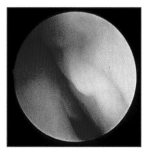

View through the lens: arthroscopy is a major surgical tool, allowing for greater accuracy of diagnosis and treatment.

arthroscopy is minimally invasive, there is a rapid post-operative return to mobility and performance.

Although arthroscopic treatment is directed primarily at treating pre-existing problems (chip fracture removal, ligament tear repair, sepsis cleansing) and does not treat osteoarthritis *per se*, it reduces the consequences of inflammatory enzyme release by removing them through a process called lavage (flushing). This helps to accelerate the return to a normal synovial environment, which is particularly important in high-motion joints, such as the fetlock and stifle.

In human medicine, arthroscopy is being used to heal damaged cartilage by incorporating the techniques of tissue engineering and cartilage replacement. While equine joint resurfacing lags behind its human counterparts, attempts at repairing cartilage have improved considerably. Although largely in the experimental stage, and with long-term studies unavailable, a few cases have been undertaken clinically. The techniques employed include:

- *Cartilage grafting* with cartilage taken from sites elsewhere in the horse and incorporated into a joint defect.
- *Synthetic grafts* have been used in human patients with knee complaints with good results. Experimental equine studies have been undertaken but do not appear superior to biological methods.
- *Mesenchymal cell transplantation* from bone marrow into arthritic joints has shown considerable promise but is presently experimental.

OTHER SURGICAL TECHNIQUES

There are several alternatives to arthroscopy that may be employed in repairing a diseased joint. Which technique is employed depends upon the presenting problem. Of the techniques described below, the first is aimed at prevention of osteoarthritis, while the remainder may be used to treat overt cases of active osteoarthritis.

PLATE/LAG SCREW FIXATION

Plate fixation and lag screw fixation are methods of fracture reconstruction so preserving the joint integrity. Examples include fractures of the cannon bone and sesamoids in racehorses.

Surgical fusion can help a return to performance in low-motion joints, such as the pastern, using lag screws or bone drilling in the hock.

Surgical fusion to save a horse (e.g for breeding stock) can be undertaken in certain high-motion joints, such as the fetlock, where medical therapies have failed or in cases where ligamentous support (i.e. suspensory ligament) has been lost.

NEURECTOMY

Neurectomy is the sectioning of nerves that supply a diseased joint. This effectively removes the ability to feel pain. The technique is generally reserved only for cases of bone spavin and navicular syndrome (osteoarthritis of the navicular area), where pain may be completely removed by nerve blocking, and where the animal is likely to return to performance following surgery.

Ethical questions are raised by this type of surgery, because there is no active attempt to cure the disease, only to remove the symptoms. Furthermore, post-operative complications and temporary responses are well documented, and these must be taken into consideration before such a procedure is undertaken.

SURGICAL FIXATION

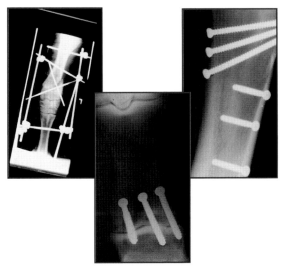

Left: Surgical fracture reconstruction.
Centre: Surgical fusion of the pastern to promote a
return to performance.
Right: Lag screw fixation of a radius.

DESMOTOMY

Desmotomy, or the sectioning of supporting
ligaments, is performed to either accelerate fusion (in
the hock), or to reduce loading and sensation (in the
navicular). Although this technique has been
undertaken in the past, it is less common today.

CONCLUSION

With any of these techniques, a successful outcome
relies heavily on careful case selection. The animal in
question must have had an accurate diagnosis made,
medical therapies at least attempted, and the owner
aware of the likely outcomes before the decision to
resort to surgical measures is taken.

6 Complementary therapies

I n recent years complementary therapies have become increasingly popular as well as becoming far more acceptable in the eyes of orthodox medicine. It is important that we do not consider these therapies purely as 'alternatives'. Rather, they should be deemed 'complementary', since this advocates a meeting of both conventional and unconventional therapies. By combining techniques, the benefits of both can be reaped and monitored.

The list of complementary therapies is forever growing longer and there is no room to include them all here. As with any treatment of any species, individual responses to each treatment can vary. Versatility and keeping an open mind (while being constructively critical) is the key to finding the best treatment for your horse.

Whatever form of complementary therapy you wish to try, it is important to ensure that the therapist you choose has the appropriate training and qualifications. You are paying for a service and you have a right to expect quality treatment. It is worth remembering that the Veterinary Surgeons Act of 1962 makes it illegal for anyone to treat an animal without authorisation from the vet in charge of a case.

PHYSIOTHERAPY

Although physiotherapy is a recognised medical therapy it is included here because of the scarcity of veterinary surgeons who offer it. In the human field, physiotherapy is used extensively in rehabilitation of muscular and skeletal problems and its benefits are well documented. Its use in veterinary medicine has been undervalued but is becoming more widespread.

Apart from osteoarthritis, physiotherapy can be used successfully to treat other common equine conditions, such as ligament and tendon injuries, back pain, and muscle imbalance or atrophy, all of which may occur in conjunction with osteoarthritis. Treatment of these concomitant problems certainly allows a more rapid return to pre-injury mobility and it has also been demonstrated most importantly in preventing injury recurrence.

Physiotherapists use a variety of techniques and combinations. Your equine physiotherapist will explain these treatments, as well as discussing treatment objectives and what results you can expect. It is also likely that you will be further advised about specific exercises you can do with your horse to aid recovery and to avoid recurrence.

CHIROPRACTY

Chiropracty deals primarily with the spinal musculo-skeletal system and the associated nerves coming from the spinal cord. A lame horse will often compensate for a painful limb by overusing the other limbs and/or altering its posture. This can create changes within the spinal musculature, restricting the normal range of motion and decreasing flexibility. Clinical signs include loss of performance, muscle spasm and stiffness.

Chiropractic treatment consists of short, sharp thrusts to specific areas, possibly by use of limb movement. This helps to release muscle spasm, alleviate pain, and help restore the joint to its normal range of motion.

However, the vast majority of back problems are secondary to a primary disease, such as osteoarthritis, with bone spavin being a typical example. This is why it is *essential* to have a veterinary surgeon diagnose the primary problem before undertaking any kind of treatment, especially chiropracty. But, with treatment for the underlying problem, there is no doubt that chiropracty can help to facilitate an early return to motion and flexibility.

Chiropractors, like physiotherapists, often advise on immediate aftercare and long-term rehabilitation.

ACUPUNCTURE

Acupuncture was first brought to Europe from China in the 17th century, and it is increasing in popularity. Traditional Chinese medicine is too complex to explain fully here, but regardless of the philosophy behind the technique and whether or not it is truly understood, there are proven scientific benefits.

The main advantage of acupuncture is its pain-killing role. This is achieved by placing needles (made of thin steel, copper, silver or gold) at various points (known as acu-points) on the horse's body. Depending on whether stimulation or suppression is required, laser treatment, injections, muscle stimulation, ultrasound, or the use of heat and cold may be used in place of needles. All these methods result in the release of natural, pain-killing hormones by the body and improved circulation. However, whether the *long-term* outcome of the disease course is altered is questionable, and many consider it unlikely.

There are many wonderful stories about the effects of acupuncture, the most astonishing of which include major operations performed on people who are fully conscious and alert as the result of placing just a few needles at the appropriate pressure points. It is also interesting that the horse's nose contains an acupuncture point – the twitching of some horses can result in their almost total relaxation.

The clinical use of acupuncture in equines is primarily for relief of muscular pain, especially over the back. However, osteoarthritis has been treated effectively by acupuncture methods. Its use in large animals is not widespread in this country although its value in small animals is becoming more appreciated, where it is used to treatment a wide range of diseases, including osteoarthritis, with very encouraging results.

The technique itself is well tolerated, although light sedation may be required in a few cases. Needles may be placed in the skin superficially or quite deep, depending on the point that needs stimulating. Each needle may stay in place for up to 10 minutes. Post-treatment, very little soreness is apparent, although human patients describe feelings ranging from nausea to euphoria. The treatment may not be exactly what you are looking for, but this therapy will certainly be far more available in the future and may come to play an important role in the treatment of equine arthritis.

RADIAL SHOCK WAVE THERAPY

Radial shock wave therapy uses 'shock waves' to treat a variety of orthopaedic conditions. The technique is relatively new but gaining in popularity.

The technique uses a high, rapid pressure wave, generated by an electric spark in a liquid medium or by pneumatic energy. The wave is emitted via an applicator, which is applied to the diseased or injured area. When a shock wave reaches the target area of tissue, a large compressive force is released. This stimulation encourages and enhances the healing process and also provides a consistent and marked reduction in pain (possibly by reducing nerve sensitivity).

In equine patients, the technique has been used in the treatment of navicular disease, fetlock osteoarthrits, and soft-tissue or muscular problems that occur with osteoarthritis. Treatment appears to be well tolerated, although light sedation may be required. There are a few mild side effects associated with the treatment, which include swelling and bleeding, but these typically resolve within 48 hours.

No complete evaluations have been carried out on the technique but anecdotal reports from practising veterinary surgeons have been promising. It is quite possible that, in the future, radial shock wave therapy could become a 'new wave' in treating equine lameness.

MAGNETIC AND ELECTROMAGNETIC THERAPY

Magnetic forces have been used for centuries, to treat everything from epilepsy to diarrhoea. Many products (generally boots and blankets) contain magnets or electromagnets, many claiming to cure every possible disease.

The most widely studied application of magnetic or electromagnetic therapy in human medicine is in fracture repair, which has received official approval in the United States. It has also been used to treat soft-tissue injuries and to relieve pain. The technique's pain-killing role has been verified in human medicine, in the treatment of osteoarthritis of the knee, spine and of the pelvis, although there are no results available from independent trials to confirm these positive results.

Equine studies have demonstrated no benefits for

healing bone or soft tissue injuries and there have been no evaluations of its use in osteoarthritis. It must be remembered that any biological organism has an innate ability to heal itself. If an injured or diseased area heals while a device touted to promote healing is applied, the device often inappropriately receives the credit. That said, anecdotal reports have described relief from osteoarthritic pain, so the therapy may become more widespread in the future.

HOMOEOPATHY

The principle of homoeopathy is one of treating like with like. The theory states that, if you treat a body with a certain substance, it will produce certain symptoms. That same substance, when given in minute quantities, will help cure those same symptoms when they are produced as the result of disease.

Exactly how homoeopathy works is unknown, although theories rebound. However, while we may not understand how or why a remedy works, that is not to say that it does not work. There are many controlled studies demonstrating the effectiveness of homoeopathy on a range of diseases, including osteoarthritis, both in humans and animals. Furthermore, there appear to be no side-effects associated with treatment, which is an obvious benefit.

There is little information available about its use in equine osteoarthritis. Future studies may reveal more practical applications for homoeopathy in equine medicine. If you are interested, ask your vet to put you in touch with someone suitable.

HERBAL MEDICINE

Herbal medicine uses plant-derived substances to treat illnesses. People have been using herbal treatments since the dawn of history. For example, it has long been recognised that White Willow bark has pain-relieving qualities. Subsequently, the compound salicylate was isolated – the active ingredient of aspirin.

Herbal medicine and orthodox medicine have a lot in common. Both use an active ingredient to treat a specific problem. The difference is that pharmaceutical medicine contains the isolated active ingredient, whereas the whole plant is used in herbal medicine.

There is no doubt that herbal medicine has highly significant benefits, but it should be remembered that, just because herbs are natural, they are not necessarily safe. There are many toxic plants, such as hemlock and ragwort. For this reason herbal medicines are licensed.

Clinical reports of use of herbal medicines in the treatment of equine osteoarthritis are lacking, but any effort to maintain an animal's overall health must be of advantage. As before, ask your vet to put you in contact with a relevant organisation if you require more information. In the UK, The British Herbal Medicine Association, although dealing primarily with human herbal medicines, should be able to help.

THE PLACEBO EFFECT

You may have noted that many of the techniques highlighted above have little conclusive evidence of their therapeutic benefit, aside from anecdotal reports from the owners. Why must we still regard some therapies with suspicion, even though clients insist it has worked?

There are many reasons for this. For example, the disease may simply have run its course, and many diseases are cyclical. Hay fever for example, only occurs in summer. Treatments may simply coincide with better days or a change in the season.

There is also the famous placebo effect. You may think this is impossible in an animal that doesn't know what it's getting, but the effect lies more with the owners, who *do* know! Research shows that up to 70 per cent of patients will report good results from techniques known to be totally ineffective – if an owner thinks it should work, it usually does. We want to believe that our animal is better. Even if no improvements are evident, rather than admitting a waste of time and money, many people will find some redeeming value in the treatment.

There remains some way to go before complementary therapies are accepted in orthodox method. However, the pages of history are littered with examples of treatment 'fashions', allegedly based on rigorous scientific examination. There is no difference today. Just as we in the veterinary profession continually question our own methods, so we must question those of others. We want to endorse therapies, but only to benefit the animal's health, not to escape accusations of obstinacy or closed-mindedness. However, even if some effects are proven to be psychological, they should not be discounted. The fact that the patient feels better is important and will have definite effects on disease, such as boosting the immune system.

The most important fact to emerge from the testing of complementary therapies is not that they are curative in their own right, but that they are 'complementary'. They are not meant to replace traditional medicine, but to allow for additional options. For example, acupuncture, osteopathy, physiotherapy, glucosamine and chondroitin supplementation, magnetic therapy, infrared therapy and massage therapy are all used in combination to alleviate and treat osteoarthritis with great success.

7 Case studies

CULLIN

Cullin was an eight-year-old Highland gelding used for general riding activities. He had not suffered from any previous lameness problems, but over a period of four weeks, Cullin's owners noticed that he was 'going short' on his left hindlimb. Examination identified a moderate lameness made worse by flexing the leg, although there were no significant abnormalities. Nerve blocks were performed on the foot, but there was no change in the degree of lameness.

Next, a local anaesthetic was injected directly into the stifle joint, and the lameness disappeared. X-rays were taken of both stifles and no abnormalities were detected. The stifle was then examined using ultrasonographic imaging to highlight the internal soft-tissue structures of the stifle, but again, no abnormalities were detected.

After discussion with the owner, Cullin received a general anaesthetic and the stifle was examined by arthroscopy. This highlighted cartilage erosion and synovial inflammation consistent with osteoarthritis. The joint was lavaged (flushed out) and Cullin given time to recover.

Following treatment, Cullin was boxed and underwent an exercise programme running over two months before being field rested for a further two months. During the first six weeks he also received a course of phenylbutazone and intramuscular polysulphated glycosaminoglycan, and received attention from a qualified physiotherapist.

Since treatment, Cullin is ridden regularly, and his exercise programme is strictly adhered to. So far, there have been no regressions.

Cullin's story demonstrates the logical diagnostic steps you may encounter with any lame horse – examination, nerve and joint blocks to identify the area of pain, followed by one of several imaging modalities. The use of arthroscopy was invaluable. It allowed direct joint visualisation, identifying the degree and severity of change, as well as providing treatment by lavage. Once diagnosis was made, other therapies (exercise management, pain relief, and medication to aid cartilage regeneration) were implemented. Importantly, exercise management was continued, despite lameness resolution, to maintain joint function and mobility and to prevent recurrence.

SKY ROCKET

Sky Rocket was an 18-month-old Thoroughbred, purchased by an owner keen to try racing. After approximately three months, a forelimb lameness was noted. Examination identified the lameness and revealed a marked fetlock effusion. The fetlock was radiographed and a chip fracture detected within the fetlock joint. These were presumed to be developmental in origin (OCD), and all four fetlocks were then X-rayed to check for further fragments. This confirmed one fetlock only was affected.

Sky was anaesthetised and arthroscopy was performed to remove the fragment and to inspect the cartilage, which was found to be largely unaffected. Post-surgery, an exercise programme was followed that included race training. Two years later, Sky has competed successfully in several races.

In this case, the important aspect was identifying

and treating the primary disorder – the chip fracture. If this had been missed, and treatment for joint effusion initiated, rapid acceleration of joint disease could have resulted. Instead, the appropriate treatment has meant complete resolution of the condition.

THOMAS

Thomas was a 12-year-old eventer/hunter, who, at the beginning of the season, was noted to be 'going short' on his near forelimb. Examination detected mild, left forelimb lameness, coffin joint and fetlock effusion, carpal thickening, and a long toe/low-heel foot conformation affecting both forefeet.

Nerve blocks isolated the pain to the foot and an intra-articular block of the coffin joint resulted in lameness resolution. X-rays highlighted enthesophyte formation in the coffin joint. The joint was medicated with a low dose of corticosteroids, and a heart-bar shoe was placed on both forefeet to correct the conformation.

After two weeks of box rest, an exercise programme was implemented. Following this, Thomas was sound, although his owner still reports problems when Thomas undertakes excessive road work or jumping. Despite this, remedial farriery is continuing and no further use of anti-inflammatory treatment has been required.

Thomas demonstrates the important consideration of foot balance. In an imbalanced foot, the forces of concussion through a limb are altered and may exacerbate or induce disease. Additionally, clinical examination detected other changes within the limb, such as fetlock effusion and carpal thickening. No horse is perfect and many problems may be found in an animal that has undertaken a lot of work. However, the nerve blocks indicated that such changes were misleading and not important in the overall picture. Furthermore, the X-ray identified changes consistent with osteoarthritis, and the joint block confirmed their significance. Finally, corticosteroids were used to achieve early mobility, while a carefully planned exercise regime avoided placing any excessive strain on an already compromised joint.

CHUKKA

Chukka was an eight-year-old Thoroughbred-cross. His owner used him for general riding activities and sought veterinary attention because Chukka had been performing poorly, knocking down poles while jumping. He was also prone to dipping when the saddle was fitted and his temperament had deteriorated.

Examination identified a moderate left hindlimb lameness and mild right hindlimb lameness. Flexion resulted in exaggeration of the lameness in both limbs. No abnormalities were found, but examination of the horse's back identified muscle pain over both hind areas of the spine. Nerve blocks were undertaken, which identified the hocks as the region of pain.

X-rays revealed changes consistent with osteoarthritis of the lower hock joints (bone spavin). Intra-articular joint anaesthesia resulted in resolution of the lameness. The joint was then treated with high-dose corticosteroids and the owner given a six-week exercise programme. A physiotherapy course was also advised. At the end of this course, the horse's lameness, demeanour and performance were markedly improved.

This final case demonstrates the need for accurate diagnosis. Back pain is a common finding in lame horses, and although the primary problem is lameness, treatment of both primary and secondary problems means a much more rapid return to work.

8 Arthritis in the future

The understanding of joint disease has come a long way since the early descriptions of the 1700s. Many of the improvements in treatment have resulted from research aimed at better understanding the process of the disease, particularly the identification of the role of inflammatory enzymes and the joint's normal response to inflammation.

Today, therapies are being developed to regulate these degradative enzymes and to stimulate repair of skeletal tissues. Molecular technology, genetic research, and surgical advances are aiding the treatments currently available, and will surely play a more important role in the future.

THE OWNER'S ROLE

To date, despite medical and surgical advances, there is no cure for osteoarthritis. While we can encourage the horse to heal itself by using orthodox medical and complementary treatments, we remain fully reliant on the animal's innate ability to heal itself.

Nevertheless, the current outlook for a horse that has arthritis is not always bleak, and results with treatment are very much influenced by you, the owner.

By caring for your horse to the best of your ability, seeking veterinary attention as soon as you notice something amiss, and following a sensible therapy plan, your horse should remain pain-free and active for many years to come.